HISTORY AND BIOGRAPHY, II

A FRIEND IN THE LIBRARY

A Practical Guide to the Writings of

RALPH WALDO EMERSON

NATHANIEL HAWTHORNE

HENRY WADSWORTH LONGFELLOW

JAMES RUSSELL LOWELL

JOHN GREENLEAF WHITTIER

OLIVER WENDELL HOLMES

IN TWELVE VOLUMES

VOLUME V

A FRIEND IN THE LIBRARY

HISTORY AND BIOGRAPHY II

BY

EVA MARCH TAPPAN

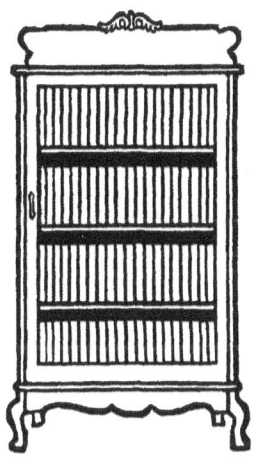

British Library Cataloguing-in-Publication Data
A catalogue record for this book is available from the
British Library

Eva March Tappan

Eva March Tappan was born on 26th December 1854 in Blackstone, Massachusetts, America. She is well known as a factual as well as fictional writer, but spent her early career as a teacher. Tappan was the only child of Reverend Edmund March Tappan and Lucretia Logée, and received her education at the esteemed Vassar College. This was a private coeducational liberal arts college, in the town of Poughkeepsie, New York, from which she graduated in 1875. Here, Tappan was a member of Phi Beta Kappa, the oldest honour society for the liberal arts and sciences, widely considered as the nations most prestigious society. She also edited the *Vassar Miscellany,* a college publication.

After leaving her early education, Tappan began teaching at Wheaton College, one of the oldest institutions of higher education for women in the United States, founded in 1834 and based in Norton, Massachusetts. She taught Latin and German here, from 1875 until 1880, before moving on to the Raymond Academy in Camden, New Jersey where she was associate Principal until 1894. Tappan also received a graduate degree in English Literature from the University of Pennsylvania. This allowed her to pursue her first love, that of reading and writing, and she taught as head of the English department at the English High School at Worcester, Massachusetts.

It was only after this date that Tappan began her literary career, writing about famous characters in history, often aimed at educating children in important historical themes and epochs. Some of her better known works include, *In the Days of William the Conqueror* (1901) and *In the Days of Queen Elizabeth* (1902), *The Out-of-Door Book* (1907), *When Knights Were Bold* (1911) and *The Little Book of the Flag* (1917). Tappan never married, being a happy singleton, and died on 29th January 1930, aged seventy-five.

HISTORY AND BIOGRAPHY, II

THE course of the government of the United States did not run very smoothly during the first years after the close of the Revolution. The states were so afraid that somebody would interfere with their liberty that they came near having no general government at all. Congress met, passed laws, and imposed taxes; but if the states did not choose to obey the laws and pay the taxes, they followed their own sweet will, and no one could oblige them to do otherwise. They were jealous of one another, and every state looked out for its rights almost as if the others had been foreign countries and enemies. Indeed, so far as opportunity for acquaintance with one another went, they might almost as well have been thousands of miles apart. It took longer to go from Boston to New York than it now takes to go from Boston to San Francisco or to England. There were no funds in the treasury, and at first no one could plan a way to get any. Most assuredly, it could not be expected that any foreign country would think of lending its money to a land in such weakness and uncertainty.

There was nothing very poetical in such a condition of affairs, and Holmes's "September Gale" (xii. 29) is quite appropriate to the general confusion. In his "Pages from an Old Volume of Life" (viii. 163), he gives a prose account of the same tempest, which occurred when he was a small boy of six years, of a "mighty howling, roaring, banging, and crashing, with much running about, and loud screaming of orders for sudden taking in of all sail about the premises, and battening down of everything that could flap or fly away." Holmes has given us a memento of the War of 1812 in his "Old Ironsides" (xii. 1). This was the pet name of the frigate Constitution, which had won so many victories in that war. It was proposed to break up the old vessel as worthless. Then it was that he wrote his poem, or, as he puts it afterwards ("Poetry," xii. 35), "Mocked the spoilers with his school-boy scorn." The poem swept over the country. It touched the sentimental American heart, and instead of being destroyed, the Constitution was thoroughly repaired and put to sea again. It is now in the Navy Yard at

Charlestown. So much for the power of a few lines of poetry.

Emerson wrote an article called "Life and Letters in New England" (x. 325), which gives a good idea of how matters intellectual were progressing in the United States in the first half of the nineteenth century. He tells of the wonderful rhetoric of Edward Everett, who brought the knowledge of European literary criticism to Cambridge, and he describes the eagerness of people to hear him. "Even the coarsest were contented to go punctually to listen, for the manner," he says, "when they had found out that the subject-matter was not for them." Emerson speaks of "The Dial," edited at first by Margaret Fuller, which "enjoyed its obscurity for four years," he declares. He speaks, too, of

Theodore Parker, "the stout Reformer to urge and defend every cause of humanity with and for the humblest of mankind." But the most interesting part of the article is his account of Brook Farm, that gilt-edged experiment in community life. An association of men and women, the majority of them of superior education, bought a large tract of land in West Roxbury and went there to live. Their theory was that they could support themselves by doing a reasonable amount of work each day, and could also have plenty of time for art, music, literature, and intellectual conversation. Emerson did not join the community, although he gave most earnest thought to the question of so doing. He did not like societies. "At the name of a society, all my repulsions play, all my quills rise and sharpen," he said.

Hawthorne lived at Brook Farm some months, and has left some valuable glimpses of the life. Milking and caring for the cows was to be part of his work. On the second day he wrote in his journal ("American Note-Books," xviii. 287), "I did not milk the cows last night, because Mr. Ripley was afraid to trust them to my hands, or me to their horns, I know not which." Then he went on to tell, a little later, what wonders he had been accomplishing as a farmer. "The Blithedale Romance" (viii.), which he wrote some years afterward, is "a faint and not very faithful shadowing of Brook Farm," he says. A letter to his sister, quoted in the Introductory Note (page xii.), gives a vivid account of his labors while trying hard to be a good member of the community. Brook Farm was no place for Hawthorne. Even when he arranged to remain there as a boarder, and was free from manual labor, the conversation and music and general ferment around him made it impossible for him to do literary work, and he soon left the place.

While these Brook Farmers were living in a little world of their own, the great world around them was moving on. The telegraph was invented, and a few years later the Atlantic Cable enabled us to communicate with Europe. That has long been an every-day matter; but in 1858 it was the marvel of the age. It touched the imagination of Whittier, and the result was his "Cable Hymn" (iv. 269) : —

> O lonely bay of Trinity,
> O dreary shores, give ear!

A FRIEND IN THE LIBRARY

> Lean down unto the white-lipped sea
> The voice of God to hear!

The success of the cable was to Whittier far
more than a convenience and an aid to business; it was the promise of world-wide peace,
and he wrote:—

> The hands of human brotherhood
> Are clasped beneath the sea!

This peace for which he hoped was not to
come at once, as Whittier well knew, for he
had been one of the leaders of the anti-slavery
movement almost from its beginning, and in
1858, when the poem was written, he must have
had small hope that war could be avoided.
He has written a most interesting account of
the Anti-Slavery Convention of 1833 ("The
Anti-Slavery Convention of 1833," vii. 171).
He was twenty-six years old when he set off

8

on the long stage-coach journey from Haverhill to Philadelphia, "better prepared for serious danger" than for the tarring and feathering of the Abolitionists, which was quite within the bounds of possibility. There were strong men present at that meeting on Fifth Street below Walnut, and Whittier has given bits of his reminiscences of them which help much to bring the scene before us. There was Garrison, whose "fine, intellectual head" rose nobly among the foremost. It was he "who had stirred the heart of the nation" in behalf of the negro. There was Samuel J. May, "the sunny-faced young man at his side"; there was the "handsome, intellectual-looking" Lewis Tappan, and his brother Arthur, who became president of the new society; there was Joshua Coffin, of whom Whittier wrote

long afterward ("To My Old Schoolmas-
ter," iv. 73) : —

> I, the urchin unto whom,
> In that smoked and dingy room,
> Where the district gave thee rule
> O'er its ragged winter school,
> Thou didst teach the mysteries
> Of those weary A, B, C's.

There were Quakers: Thomas Shipley,
"whose name was whispered reverently in
the slave-cabins of Maryland as the friend of
the black man"; and Lucretia Mott, "with a
face beneath her plain cap as finely intellectual as that of Madame Roland." To many of
these leaders Whittier pays in other volumes
of his works the warmest tributes of love and
admiration. Lowell has written with eager
praise of Wendell Phillips, who scorned the

gifts of "fame, and power, and gold," and "humbly joined him to the weaker part." Longfellow writes of Sumner (iii. 83) : —

> So when a great man dies,
> For years beyond our ken,
> The light he leaves behind him lies
> Upon the paths of men.

But the anti-slavery leaders had small thought of poetical tributes to come. In 1844 the whole land was discussing the annexation of Texas, with the consequent increase of slavery. Then it was that Lowell wrote his "Present Crisis" (ix. 185), with its keen sword-thrust : —

> Once to every man and nation comes the moment to decide,
> In the strife of Truth with Falsehood, for the good or evil side.

Six years later was the date of the Missouri Compromise and the Fugitive Slave Law. This was supported by Daniel Webster. It was of this act of his that Whittier wrote his stern and sorrowful "Ichabod" (iv. 61), keeping in mind the Hebrew meaning of the word, *the glory has departed.* This closes: —

> Then, pay the reverence of old days
>   To his dead fame;
> Walk backward with averted gaze,
>   And hide the shame!

Emerson rarely spoke on public questions — he had his own "spirits in prison," he said; but on the fourth anniversary of Webster's Seventh of March speech in favor of the Fugitive Slave Law, Emerson delivered an address (xi. 218), in which is an appreciative picture of the great orator's ability, and an earnest expression of his own grief and surprise that such a man should have given the casting vote in favor of the law.

Soon after the passing of this law, Franklin Pierce was nominated for President of the United States. He was an early friend of Hawthorne's, and the romancer was asked to write his life to serve as a campaign document. This was a task which Hawthorne frankly declared was not to his taste; but his dislike yielded to his friendship, and he wrote the book (xvii. 75). It gives a good idea of Pierce's character and attainments, and describes his services to the country in peace and his noble bravery in war. It reveals a sincere friendship and admiration on the part of Hawthorne; but he was out of his element. It is not easy to write the life of a person who will certainly read the work, and for a man as sensitive as he it was doubly difficult. An ordinary mortal might be proud of having produced so clearly and pleasantly written a biography; but there is little if anything in it that could add to the reputation of Hawthorne.

A few years later, after, as Holmes said, a civil request that the nation "would commit suicide without making any unnecessary trouble about it" ("The Inevitable Trial," viii. 78), warfare began. Not much more than a year had passed when he was aroused at midnight by the ring of a telegraphic messenger. "Capt. H—— wounded shot through the neck thought not mortal at Keedysville," said the message. "Capt. H——" was Holmes's dearly beloved son; and soon he was hurrying through Philadelphia, Frederick, and

Middletown to Keedysville, in search of the wounded soldier. The search was almost like that of Evangeline for Gabriel done into nineteenth-century circumstances. "The Captain" had been seen by one and heard of by another — in some place where he could not possibly have been at the time named; telegrams missed fire, — some lines were serving the government and could not be used for any private business. But Holmes himself must tell ("My Hunt after 'The Captain,'" viii. 16) what lies between the arrival of the telegram and the very nineteenth-century greeting,

"How are you, Boy?"
"How are you, Dad?"

which brought the golden ending to the story.

While Holmes was searching for "the Captain," weighty deeds were being done in

Washington: the Emancipation Proclamation declared that three months later all slaves
in states that had not then returned to their
allegiance should be forever free. On the day
when this Proclamation went into force,
Emerson's "Boston Hymn" (ix. 201) was
read in Music Hall. This begins:—

> The word of the Lord by night
> To the watching Pilgrims came,
> As they sat by the seaside,
> And filled their hearts with flame.

Closely following on the end of the war came
the murder of Lincoln, an equal loss to North
and to South. The fine eulogy in Lowell's
"Commemoration Ode" has been mentioned
elsewhere; but Emerson's brief remarks on
his character at the memorial service held in
Concord ("Abraham Lincoln," xi. 327) are

worth reading for their perfect comprehension and appreciation of this man of the people.

The war had come to an end in 1865. Four years later, a musical "Jubilee" was held in Boston to mark the return of peace, with music of voice and instrument. Bands from England, France, and Germany were aided by an orchestra of two thousand musicians and a chorus of twenty thousand voices. Not all who attended the Jubilee were musical geniuses, and it is quite probable that hundreds at least were less impressed by any other number on the programme than by the Anvil Chorus, rendered, so far as the anvil music comes in, by firemen in red shirts, with real hammers and real anvils. One enthusiastic hearer exclaimed that it "seemed like the first taste of heaven"; and she was perhaps not so far from the truth when one remembers that this Jubilee marked the "peace beginning to be" of a mighty nation. Holmes was called upon to write a "Hymn of Peace" (xiii. 147) for the occasion. This is its first stanza: —

Angel of Peace, thou hast wandered too long!
  Spread thy white wings to the sunshine of love!
Come while our voices are blended in song, —
  Fly to our ark like the storm-beaten dove!

Not all was peace, however. In our centennial year, 1876, occurred the war with the Sioux in which General Custer and every one of his followers were slain.

Into the fatal snare
The White Chief with yellow hair
  And his three hundred men
Dashed headlong, sword in hand;
But of that gallant band
  Not one returned again.

So wrote Longfellow in his "Revenge-in-the-Face" (iii. 111). Ten years later, the fierce chieftain applied to enter the Hampton School as a learner. Of this, Whittier wrote ("On the Big Horn," iii. 371) : —

> O Hampton, down by the sea!
> What voice is beseeching thee
>   For the scholar's lowliest place?
> Can this be the voice of him
> Who fought by the Big Horn's rim?
>   Can this be Rain-in-the-Face?
>
> His war-paint is washed away,
> His hands have forgotten to slay;
>   He seeks for himself and his race
> The arts of peace and the lore
> That give to the skilled hand more
>   Than the spoils of war and chase.

The close of our first century of independence was marked by the Centennial Exposition. Holmes was called upon to extend greeting to the many nations represented ("Welcome to the Nations," xiii. 174), and Whittier to write a hymn for the opening of the exhibition. This was his reverent and dignified "Centennial Hymn" (iv. 205) with its noble beginning: —

> Our fathers' God! from out whose hand
> The centuries fall like grains of sand, —
> We meet to-day, united, free,
> And loyal to our land and Thee,
> To thank Thee for the era done,
> And trust Thee for the opening one.

One of the most delightful characteristics of the life of the literary men of America in the nineteenth century was their almost unvarying lack of jealousy and their full appreciation of one another's work. After the young Motley had decided to write a history of the Dutch

Republic, he learned that Prescott was occupied with so closely connected a subject that the two works would clash. As Motley said, he had not first made up his mind to write and then looked about him for a theme; he had become so intensely interested in that one subject that to give it up was like renouncing all thought of authorship. He went frankly to the older author, and Prescott met him with warm-hearted sympathy and offered the use of his library. "No two books ever injure each other," he declared, and gave the young writer the most cordial encouragement. When his own "Philip the Second" was published, behold, there was in the preface a note speaking most highly of Motley's ability and recommending his history which was soon to come out. Holmes tells this story in his "John

Lothrop Motley" (xi. 327), one of the two biographies that he wrote. He remembered well the handsome boy of thirteen who entered Harvard with a reputation for being a "wonderful linguist"; and from his own memories and those of Motley's classmates he brings the future historian before us most vividly. A letter which Holmes quotes from Thomas G. Appleton speaks of him as sometimes writing verses for the "Anti-Masonic Mirror," in the corner of which paper was a woodcut of Apollo, "inviting to destruction ambitious youths by the legend underneath,

Much yet remains unsung."

Holmes tells us of the days when the college boy Motley used to write a drawerful of sketches, plays, and poems, burn them up, and set to work to fill the drawer again; then of the time when Motley, at the end of his ten years' labor on the history, carried his manuscript to a famous English publisher, and found it "declined with thanks." He brought it out at his own expense; and it was so successful that the famous publisher meekly asked to be allowed to bring out his next work. The historian's diplomatic career also is faithfully described. Holmes had most excellent material for the story of Motley's life; but a dull man with an equally full storehouse to draw from would only have produced something as dull as himself. This biography is interesting from beginning to end.

Holmes's second biographical work was a life of Emerson (xi. 1). He brings before us clearly the "spiritual-looking boy in blue nankeen," and the "captive philosopher set to tending flocks," as he appeared during his pedagogic days. There were so few striking incidents in Emerson's career that his biographer is forced to tell the story of his intellectual life, whether he will or not. Holmes has done this most wisely by using as far as possible Emerson's own words, quotations from his essays and letters. Holmes is always Holmes, and even in the biography of a philosopher, he cannot hide his sense of the humorous. He quotes Emerson's, "You shall not come nearer a man by getting into his house," and queries mischievously, "What would have been the issue if Carlyle had come to Concord and taken up his abode under Emerson's most hospitable roof? 'Come rest in this bosom,' is a sweet air, heard in the distance," Holmes declares, but "too apt to be followed, after a protracted season of close proximity, by that other strain, —

> No, fly me, fly me, far as pole from pole!
> Rise Alps between us and whole oceans roll!"

Where Holmes gives original criticism, it is of course most excellent, especially when he talks of Emerson's poems. He points out the " desperate work" that the philosopher sometimes made with rhyme and rhythm. He demands, "How could prose go on all-fours more unmetrically than this?

> In Adirondack lakes
> At morn or noon the guide rows bare-headed!

It was surely not difficult to say —

> At morn or noon bare-headed rows the guide."

But, says Holmes, "When he is at his best, his lines flow with careless ease, as a mountain stream tumbles, sometimes rough and sometimes smooth, but all the more interesting for the rocks it runs against and the grating of the pebbles it rolls over." He says that Emerson was a cautious mystic, who "never let go the string of his balloon." And, descending from metaphysical to gaseous balloons, it is interesting to note that the mystic Emerson predicts, "We are to have the balloon yet, and the next war will be fought in the air"; while the scientist Holmes thus annotates the prophecy: "Possibly; but it is perhaps as safe to predict that it will be fought on wheels; the soldiers on bicycles, the officers on tricycles." The whole sketch of Emerson is marked by a tender appreciation of the man and his works. Holmes says in closing: —

Whether it [Emerson's best literary work] live or fade from memory, the influence of his great and noble life, and the spoken and written words which were its exponents, blends, indestructible, with the enduring elements of civilization.

So it is that the really great authors spoke of one another, feeling no envy, but rather the warmest appreciation of one another's work and the most sincere pleasure in one another's success. Each was ready with tongue and pen to express his joy in whatever good fortune came to any one of the number, or at the coming of any sorrow to send the word of sympathy that made the grief easier to bear. Birthday greetings, farewells, and welcomings, slipped gracefully from the pens of these friends. On Whittier's seventieth birthday Holmes wrote ("For Whittier's Seventieth Birthday," xiii. 222) his song of good cheer : —

The wood-thrush of Essex, — you know whom I mean,
Whose song echoes round us while he sits unseen,
Whose heart-throbs of verse through our memories
    thrill
Like a breath from the wood, like a breeze from the
    hill.

Two years later, the publishers of the "Atlantic Monthly" gave a breakfast in honor of the "Autocrat," and for this Whittier wrote "Our Autocrat" (xiii. 142), with its kindly—

> Though now unnumbered guests surround
>   The table that he rules at will,
> Its Autocrat, however crowned,
>   Is but our friend and comrade still.

The band of friends was soon broken. Hawthorne was the first to go. It was in memory of the day of his burial that Longfellow wrote his "Hawthorne" (iii. 137), which closes, —

Ah! who shall lift that wand of magic power,
And the lost clue regain?
The unfinished window in Aladdin's tower
Unfinished must remain!

Even more tenderly did Whittier write of Longfellow in his "The Poet and the Children" (iv. 150), the familiar verses that begin,

With a glow of winter sunshine
Over his locks of gray,
In the old historic mansion
He sat on his last birthday.

Many years before this, Holmes had written on the departure of Longfellow for Europe ("To H. W. Longfellow," xiii. 103), —

Where shall the singing bird a stranger be
That finds a nest for him in every tree?
How shall he travel who can never go
Where his own voice the echoes do not know,
Where his own garden flowers no longer learn to grow?

Longfellow died in 1882; Lowell in 1891; Whittier one year later. It was of Lowell that Holmes wrote ("James Russell Lowell," xiii. 331), —

Thou shouldst have sung the swan-song for the choir
  That filled our grove with music.

Whittier's last poem was his "To Oliver Wendell Holmes" (iv. 315). A few weeks after it was written, the playful prophecy of Holmes's early poem, "The Last Leaf" (xii. 3), had been fulfilled, and Holmes had become "the last leaf upon the tree."

These good friends, and others of the literary "great folk," formed the Saturday Club, whose vitality "depended in a great measure on its utter poverty in statutes and by-laws, its entire absence of formality, and its blessed freedom from speech-making" (Holmes, xi.

497). Holmes has written of it in verse half serious and half playful ("At the Saturday Club," xiii. 267), and in his life of Emerson (xi. 1) he has given the following prose account of it:—

The club seems to have shaped itself around him [Emerson] as a nucleus of crystallization, two or three friends of his having first formed the habit of meeting him at dinner at "Parker's," the "Will's Coffee-House" of Boston. This little group gathered others to itself and grew into a club as Rome grew into a city, almost without knowing how. During its first decade, the Saturday Club brought together, as members or visitors, many distinguished persons. At one end of the table sat Longfellow, florid, quiet, benignant, soft-voiced, a most agreeable rather than a brilliant talker, but a man upon whom it was always pleasant to look, — whose silence was better than many another man's conversation. At the other end of the table sat Agassiz, robust, sanguine, animated, full of talk, boy-like in his laughter. The stranger who might have asked who were the men ranged along the sides of the table would have heard in answer the names of Hawthorne, Motley, Dana, Lowell, Whipple, Pierce, the distinguished mathematician, Judge Hoar, eminent at the bar and in the cabinet, Dwight, the leading musical critic of Boston for a whole generation, Sumner, the academic champion of Freedom, Andrew, the great "War Governor" of Massachusetts, Dr. Howe, the philanthropist, William Hunt, the painter, with others not unworthy of such company.

If there were only a record of those "Golden hours!"

HISTORY AND BIOGRAPHY

ADDITIONAL

HAWTHORNE

Biographical Stories, xii. 265.
Biographical Sketches, xvii. 1.

EMERSON

Representative Men, iv.
Lectures and Biographical Sketches, x. 379.
Miscellanies, xi.
Natural History of Intellect, xii. 213, 337.

WHITTIER

To W. L. Garrison, iii. 9, 269.
The Lost Occasion, iv. 63.
Wordsworth, iv. 66.
Bayard Taylor, iv. 140.
In Memory: James T. Fields, iv. 146.
Chicago, iv. 195.
Portraits and Sketches, vi.

LONGFELLOW

President Garfield, iii. 321.
Santa Filomena, iii. 50.

The Discoverer of the North Cape, iii. 52.
The Fiftieth Birthday of Agassiz, iii. 57.
Bayard Taylor, iii. 266.
The Children's Crusade, iii. 304.

HOLMES

Over the Teacups, iv., contains many biographical anecdotes.
Brother Jonathan's Lament for Sister Caroline, xii. 284.
Bryant's Seventieth Birthday, xiii. 92.
A Farewell to Agassiz, xiii. 96.
Edward Everett, xiii. 113.
Our Dead Singer, H. W. L., xiii. 273.
To James Russell Lowell, xiii. 281.

LOWELL

Garfield, vii. 39.
Stanley, vii. 51.
Wendell Phillips, ix. 73.
To W. L. Garrison, ix. 289.
To H. W. L., xii. 285.
Agassiz, xiii. 111.
To Holmes on His Seventy-fifth Birthday, xiii. 130.

HISTORY AND BIOGRAPHY

QUESTIONS

1. Why has no more literature been written
   about the early days of our Republic?
   *Because its weakness and uncertainty
   afforded poor subjects for literature.*

2. What is the most famous poem connected
   with the War of 1812?
   Holmes's "Old Ironsides" (xii. 2).

3. What does this poem illustrate?
   The power of a few lines of poetry.

4. Why is Emerson's "Life and Letters in New
   England" so valuable?
   *Because it gives so excellent a picture of the
   progress of literature in New England,*

35

and describes so interestingly the Brook Farm experiment.

5. What novel is based in some degree upon the life of Brook Farm?
   Hawthorne's "Blithedale Romance."

6. What poem celebrates the laying of the Atlantic Cable?
   Whittier's "Cable Hymn."

7. Why did the Cable touch his imagination?
   Because it seemed to him to promise a world-wide peace.

8. In what movement was Whittier most deeply interested?
   In the anti-slavery movement.

9. Which article of his anti-slavery writings is of special historical value?
   The Anti-Slavery Convention of 1833.

10. What poem was the outgrowth of the discussion concerning the annexation of Texas?
    Lowell's "Present Crisis" (ix. 185).

11. What poem is associated with the Fugitive Slave Law?

    Whittier's "Ichabod" (iv. 61).

12. Why does the life of Franklin Pierce (xvii. 75) add nothing to Hawthorne's literary fame?

    Because romance and not biography was his element.

13. What sketch illustrates the confusion of war times?

    Holmes's "My Hunt after 'the Captain'" (viii. 16).

14. What poem was read to a large audience in Boston to celebrate the Emancipation Proclamation?

    Emerson's "Boston Hymn" (ix. 201).

15. What was the origin of Holmes's "Hymn of Peace" (xiii. 147)?

    It was written for the Peace Jubilee of 1869.

16. Who wrote the "Centennial Hymn" (iv. 105) for the opening of our Centennial Exposition?

    Whittier.

17. What was the feeling of the literary men of the second half of the nineteenth century toward one another?

    Most cordial and appreciative.

18. How do the two biographies written by Holmes differ in treatment?

    That of Motley pays more attention to events; that of Emerson to its subject's intellectual life.

19. Why is Holmes's "Last Leaf" (xii. 3) called a prophecy?

    Because Holmes lived longest of "the choir."

20. What was the Saturday Club?

    An informal club of men of letters and achievements who dined together once a month.

www.ingramcontent.com/pod-product-compliance
Lightning Source LLC
Chambersburg PA
CBHW020919180626
46816CB00007BA/2487